Top's and Yo-Yo's
And Other Spinning Toys

©1995
L-W Book Sales

ISBN#: 0-89538-037-4

Published by: L-W Book Sales
              PO Box 69
              Gas City, IN 46933

Please write for our free catalog.

Attention Collectors...if you would like to contribute photographs or information of your collection (possibly for profit), please call L-W Books (toll free) at 1-800-777-6450 Tuesday thru Friday 9am to 3pm.

Preface

In today's collectible market, many antique genres as of late have been overshadowed by the tremendous gathering of TOYS. Pioneer wooden toys, old metal toys, and Baby Boomer era playthings have begun to dominate more than their fair share of the collectible spotlight. Toys generate untold emotions among the collector - joy, amusement, and wonder - not to mention a nostalgic longing for childhood, unimpaired by either conscience or responsibility. The toys portrayed in this volume - tops and yo-yos - have emerged as collectible keepsakes of generations both young and old.

For over 4,000 years, children the world over have been enthralled and entertained by the "mysterious" spinning toy - the top. Even in today's modernistic lifestyle, children marvel at the dizzying device just as youngsters did during the Ancient Egyptian and Sumerian civilizations. As the premise of the top's operation is merely fundamental physics, it has assumed many forms throughout its development depending on materials used and the construction method utilized. As the construction of a top must always be symmetrical in shape, most variations among toys of this type are the colorful patterns embellished upon its outer frame. Due to its spiralling motion, a variety of illusions may be discovered in a dazzling display with a simple spin of a vibrantly patterned top.

Yo-yos may not have as illustrious of a history as its cousin the top, but Americans have wholeheartedly adopted yo-yos into contemporary American culture nonetheless. A United States trademark incorporating the yo-yo was recorded in 1932, yet similar toys bearing the same name have been seen in the Phillipines as early as 1915. As such, the yo-yo is so far of an undetermined origin. A simple spool-like contraption with an attached string, the yo-yo is intended to ascend and descend using a simple flick of the wrist as the string is held and the yo-yo is left to dance merrily above the floor, seemingly defying gravity with every graceful swoop. Apparently a rather elementary device, a generous amount of manual dexterity must be applied in order to master its motion, not to mention the hundreds of tricks yo-yo "professionals" have developed over decades past. The yo-yo enjoyed its height of popularity during the 1950's & 1960's, but even today they can be found at virtually every toy store or nestled in the bottom of a toy box near you.

The prevalence of the top and the yo-yo throughout the last century has provided a wealth of available treasures out there, just waiting to be had. Garage sales, rummages, auctions, and flea markets should yield a decent handful or two of enviable items, while the more colorful or unusual specimens may have already hustled their way into an antique dealer's showcase or a booth at an antique mall, particularly those specializing in the collectible toy field. Where ever your search may begin, you will enjoy your spin throughout the realm of the whirling, twirling dynasty of tops and yo-yos.

Table of Contents

Finger Tops 5-10

Peg Tops 11-17

Tops with Spinners 18-27

Advertising Tops 28-36

Larger Plunger Tops 37-52

Top Related Items 53-56

Wooden Yo-Yos 57-60

Metal Yo-Yos 61-62

Plastic Yo-Yos 63-65

Duncan Yo-Yos 66-75

Wood & Metal Advertising Yo-Yos 76-78

Plastic Advertising Yo-Yos 79-88

Character Yo-Yos 89-96

Yo-Yo Related Items 97-101

Gyros 102-106

Miscellaneous Spinning Toys 107-112

Finger Tops

Above: Wooden Finger Top
5 1/2" Dia.
{Note Painted Surface}
$20

Left: Modern Japanese Finger Top
2 1/2" x 1 1/2" Dia.
$15

Right: Enameled Wooden Finger Top
3" x 2 1/2" Dia.
{Note Enameled Surface and Heavy
Wood Construction}
$10

Right: Wooden Finger Top
1 1/2" Dia. x 2"
{Note: Hand-Painted}
$25

Left: Ro-To-Top
(Cast iron w/ wood handle)
4" x 2 1/2" Dia.
{Note: Model or Casting #10}
$15

Right: Wooden English Top
1" Dia.
$10

Left: Top for "Put & Take"
Game
Wood w/ Paper Label
2" x 1" Dia.
$10

Left: Wooden Figural Finger Top
2" x 1 1/4" Dia.
$10

Right: Wooden Figural Finger Top
1 1/2" x 3/4" Dia.
$10

Left: Wooden Finger Top
2 1/2" Dia. x 3 1/2"
$15

Right: Wooden Finger Top
5/8" Dia. x 1"
$10

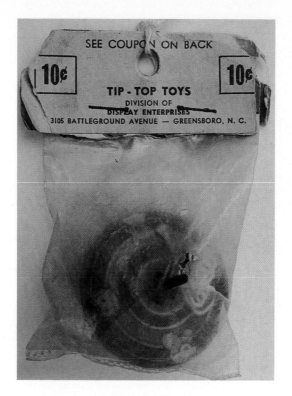

Above: Tin Top in Original Packaging
(Tip Top Toys)
{Note: Coupon Has Been Removed}
$15 in package

Above: Tin Finger Top
2 3/4" x 4" Dia.
{Note Ringing Action with Loose Bearing Inside}
$15

Left: Plastic "Santa" Finger Top
(Shackman Co., 1984)
3/4" x 1 1/2" Dia.
$5

Right: Plastic "Santa" Finger Top
(Shackman Co., 1984)
3/4" x 1 1/2" Dia.
$5

Left: Plastic "Santa" Finger Top
(Shackman Co., 1984)
3/4" x 1 1/2" Dia.
$5

Right: Plastic "Santa" Finger Top
(Shackman Co., 1984)
3/4" x 1 1/2" Dia.
$5

Above: Tiny Tin Tops
(Originally offered as Cracker Jack prizes; Made in Japan)
13/16" Dia.
$10 each

Left: Plastic "Baseball
Pitching" Top
1 1/4" Dia.
$5

Right: Wooden Finger Top
1 3/4" Dia. x 2"
{Note Painted Surface}
$5

Peg Tops

Above: Plastic Peg Top
(Imperial Toy Corp.; 1973;
Made in Hong Kong)
1 1/2" x 1" Dia.
$5

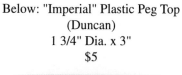

Below: "Imperial" Plastic Peg Top
(Duncan)
1 3/4" Dia. x 3"
$5

Left: Plastic Peg Top
2 1/2" x 1 1/2" Dia.
{Note Brass Peg}
$5

Right: Plastic Peg Top
2" Dia. x 3"
{Note Metal Tip}
$5

Left: Plastic "Whizzer" Top
(Mattel, Inc.; 1969)
2" Dia. x 3"
$10

Right: "Chicago Twister"
Spinning Top
(Duncan)
1 3/4" Dia. x 2 1/2"
{Note: On Top it Reads
"Duncan Tornado"}
$20 on card

Left: "Tournament"
Spinning Top
(Duncan)
3" x 2" Dia.
$25 on card

Above: Wooden Peg Tops w/ Metal Tips
Left: 2 1/4" x 1 1/2" Dia.
$5
Middle: 2 5/8" x 1 1/2" Dia.
$5
Right: 2 1/2" x 2" Dia.
$5

Above: Wooden Peg Tops w/ Ball Bearing Tips
1 1/2" Dia. x 2 1/2"
$10 each

Above: Pair of Wooden Peg Top "Whistlers"
(Duncan)
2 1/2" x 2" Dia.
$15

Left: Hollow Wooden Top
2" x 2" Dia.
{Note Plastic Tip}
$15

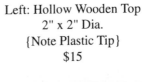

Right: Wooden "Kidstuff" Top
(Fli-Back)
2" Dia. x 3"
$5

Left: Wooden Peg Top
2 1/2" x 1 1/2" Dia.
{Note Metal Tip}
$5

Right: Hand-DecoratedWooden Top
2" x 1 1/2" Dia.
{Note: Flat Tip}
$5

Wooden Peg Top
2 1/4" x 1 1/2" Dia.
$5

Above: Wooden Peg Tops
2 1/2" x 1 1/2" Dia.
$5 each

Below: Wooden Peg Top
2" Dia. x 4"
{Note Natural Grain Surface}
$10

Above: Wooden Peg Top w/ Ball Bearing Tip
3" x 2 1'2" Dia.
$10

Left: Wooden Peg Top
3" x 2 1/2" Dia.
$5

Left: Wooden Peg Top
3 1/2" x 2 1/2" Dia.
{Note Lengthy Metal Peg}
$15

Right: Wooden Peg Top
2 1/2" x 1 1/2" Dia.
$10

Left: Plastic "Imperial" Peg Top
(Duncan)
1 3/4" Dia. x 3")
$10

Right: Wooden Peg Top
1 1/2" x 1 1/8" Dia.
$5

Tops with Spinners

Left: Wooden Top w/ Stringed Launch Bracket (Imprint reads "Patented July of 1899) 4" x 2 1/4" Dia. $100+

Right: Wooden Top w/ Stringed Launch Bracket (Made in Czech Republic) 3 3/4" x 1 1/2" Dia. $15

Left: Tin Litho Top w/ Stringed Launch Bracket 1 1/2" Dia. x 1 1/2" $15

Right: Tin Litho Top w/ Stringed Launch Bracket 1 1/2" Dia. x 1 1/2" $15

Left: Plastic Top w/
Wooden Hand Launcher
4" Dia. x 3 1/2"
$5

Below: Tin Top w/ Wooden
Hand Launcher
1 1/2" Dia. x 2 1/2"
$10

Above: Glass & Metal Top w/ Wooden
Hand Launcher
1 1/2" Dia. x 4"
$40

Right: Tin Litho Top w/
Wooden Hand
Launcher
3 1/2" Dia. x 4 1/2"
$25

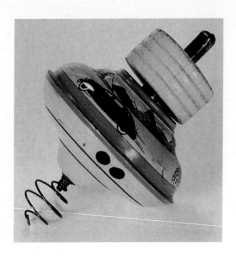

Left: Tin Top w/ Wooden
Hand Launcher
1 1/2" Dia. x 2 1/2"
$10

Right: Tin Top w/
Wooden Hand Launcher
2" Dia. x 2 1/2"
$10

Left: Tin "Carousel" Top w/
Wooden Hand Launcher
3" Dia. x 3"
$15

Tin Litho Top w/ Wood &
Metal Hand Launcher
(Made in Japan)
4" x 3" Dia.
{Note Springs on Bottom}
$20

Tin Litho Top w/ Wooden
Hand Launcher
4" Dia. x 4"
$15

Right: Tin Litho Top w/
Wooden Hand Launcher
(Ohio Art)
5" Dia. x 4"
$10

Left: Tin Litho Top w/
Wooden Hand Launcher
(Made in Japan)
4" x 3" Dia.
{Note Western Litho Design
& Springs on Bottom}
$15

Right: Tin Litho Top
w/ Hand Launcher
(Made in Japan)
5" Dia. x 3 1/2"
$30

Left: "Improved Mechanical
Spring Top" Tin Top w/ Tin
Hand Launcher
2" Dia. x 4"
$40

Right: Tin Litho Top w/ Metal
Spring Launcher
1 1/2" Dia. x 1 1/2"
$15

Left: Tin Litho Tops w/ Tin
Hand Launcher
(Made in Japan)
2 1/2" Dia. x 3"
{Note Springs on Bottom}
$10

Right: Tin Litho Top w/ Tin
Hand Launcher
(Made in Korea)
2" Dia. x 2 1/4"
$10

Above: Tin Litho "Music Spring Top" Display
(ICS Trademark)
Tops: 1 1/2" x 1 1/2" Dia.; Display: 8 1/2" x 6 1/2"
$60 with display

Left: Tin Litho Top w/ Tin
Hand Launcher
(Lindstrom)
3" Dia. x 3"
$15

Right: Tin Litho "Gibe Toy" Top
w/ Tin Hand Launcher
3" Dia. x 3 1/2"
$10

Above: Tin Litho Top w/ Tin Hand Launcher
(Made in Japan)
2 1/2" Dia. x 3"
$10

Left: Tiny Tin Top w/ Metal
Hand Launcher
2 1/2" x 1 1/2" Dia.
{Note Release is on Stem;
Marked "C.P." on Top}
$30

Right: Tin Litho Top w/
Metal Hand Launcher
2 1/2" Dia. x 2 1/2"
{Note Bouncing Spring
on Bottom}
$10

Right: Tin Top w/
Metal Hand Launcher
4" Dia. x 4"
$40

Left: Tin Top w/ Metal
Launcher
(Made in Germany by MNN)
2" Dia. x 3 1/4"
$60

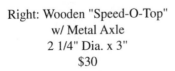

Right: Wooden "Speed-O-Top"
w/ Metal Axle
2 1/4" Dia. x 3"
$30

Above: Press Lever Top Set
(Louis Marx & Co.)
Tops: 2" Dia. x 2 3/4"
$200+ with box

Above: Large English Wooden "Humming" Top
3" Dia. x 7"
{Note: Holes on Sides Create Whistling Noise When Spinning}
$50

Advertising Tops

Left: Tin & Wood Finger Top
[Aid Assoc. for Lutherans]
(Parisian Novelty Co.)
1 1/4" Dia.
$25

Right: Wood & Celluloid
Finger Top
[Alms & Doepke Toyland]
1 1/2" Dia.
$20

Left: Tin & Wood Finger Top
[Betsy Ross Bread]
1 1/2" Dia.
$30

Right: Metal & Wood
"Baseball" Top
[Buckingham's, 1918]
1 1/2" Dia.
$35

Left: Tin & Wood
Finger Top
[Buster Brown Shoes]
$35

Right: Plastic Finger Top
[Jimmy Carter Pres.
Campaign, 1976]
1 1/2" Dia.
$5

Above: Plastic Finger Tops
[Coca-Cola, 1970's]
$20 each

Right: Tin & Wood Finger Top
[Cracker Jack]
1 1/2" Dia.
$45

Left: Steel & Wood Finger Top
[Derby Products]
(Parisian Novelty Co.)
1 1/4" Dia.
$25

Right: Wood & Celluloid
Finger Top
[DeVries & Dornbos]
(Patricia Novelty Co.)
1 1/4" Dia.
$30

Left: Steel & Wood
Finger Top
[E-A-Co Flour]
(Parisian Novelty Co.)
1 1/4" Dia.
$45

Right: Tin & Wood "Ouija" Top
[Earl Motor Car]
$35

Left: Wood & Celluloid Finger Top
[Favorite Stoves & Ranges]
1 1/2" Dia.
$45

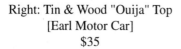

Right: Plastic Finger Top
[New Ford Falcon/ Auto Sales]
(Salesman Sample)
$15

31

Left: Tin & Wood Finger Top
[Geo. Innes Co.]
(Parisian Novelty Co.)
1 1/2" Dia.
$30

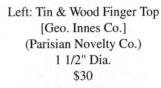

Right: Steel & Wood Finger Top
[Homestead Loan & Savings]
(Parisian Novelty Co.)
1 1/4" Dia.
$25

Left: Plastic Finger Top
[McDonald's]
2 1/2" Dia. x 2"
$10

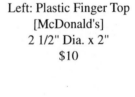

Right: Tin & Wood Finger Top
[Pittsburgh Plate Glass Co.]
1 1/4" Dia.
$50

Left: Tin & Wood Finger Top
[Pluto Water]
$45

Right: Tin & Wood Finger Top
[Plymouth Tip-Top Used Cars]
$40

Left: Wooden Peg Top
[Poll Parrot Shoes]
1" Dia. x 1 1/2"
{Note Metal Tip}
$30

Right: Tin & Wood Finger Top
[Poll Parrot Shoes]
1 1/2" Dia.
$15

Left: Wood & Celluloid Finger Top
[Q-R-S Music Co.]
1 1/2" Dia.
$35

Right: Tin & Wood Finger Top
[Red Goose Shoes]
1 1/2" Dia.
$45

Left: Wood & Metal Finger Top
[Sanitary Farm Dairies]
1" Dia. x 1"
$30

Right: Tin Top w/ Aluminum
Hand Launcher
[Silver Top Ale]
1 1/2" Dia. x 2 1/2"
$45

Left: Tin & Wood Finger Top
[Spinners Gum]
$25

Right: Tin & Wood Finger Top
[Tastykake]
(Kirchhof)
1 1/2" Dia.
$20

Left: Tin & Wood Finger Top
[Tastykake]
(Parisian Novelty Co.)
$25

Right: Tin & Wood "Ouija" Top
[Thom McAn Shoes]
$40

Left: Plastic Finger Top
[Trix Cereal]
1" Dia.
$10

Left: Tin & Wood Finger Top
[Vanta Baby Garments]
$25

Right: Tin & Wood Finger Top
[Weatherbird Shoes]
1 3/8" Dia.
$25

Left: Tin, Wood & Celluloid Finger Top
[W.O.W. - Woodmen of the World]
1 1/2" Dia.
$20

Right: Wood & Celluloid Finger
Top
[Wurzburg]
(Patricia Novelty Co.)
1 1/4" Dia.
$20

Large "Plunger" Tops

Left: Tin & Wood
"Peanuts" Top
(J. Chein & Co.; 1969)
10" x 6"
$30

Right: Tin & Plastic
"Snoopy & the Gang" Top
(Ohio Art; 1966)
6" x 6" Dia.
$30

Left: Tin & Wood
"Shirt Tales" Top
(Ohio Art; 1982)
7" x 6 1/2"
$5

Right: Tin & Wood "Mickey
Mouse & Friends" Top
10" Dia. x 11"
$200+

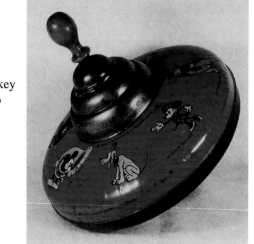

Left: Tin & Wood Mickey Mouse
& the Band Top
(Fritz Bueschel; Made in USA)
7" Dia. x 7"
$200+

Right: Tin Litho & Wood
Mickey Mouse Top
(Straco; 1978)
6 3/4" Dia. x 5 3/4"
$20

Left: Tin & Wood
Nursery Rhyme Top
(J. Chein & Co.)
6 1/2" Dia. x 6"
$20

Right: Tin & Wood
"Three Little Pigs"
Top
(Ohio Art)
$40 with box

Left: Tin & Wood "Ten
Little Indians" Top
(Ohio Art)
7 1/2" x 6 1/2"
$30

Above: Tin & Wood "Mulberry Bush" Top
(Ohio Art)
6 1/2" Dia. x 7"
$25

Above: Tin & Wood "Three Little Pigs on a Carousel" Top
(J. Chein & Co.)
6 3/4" Dia. x 6 1/2"
$35

Left: Tin & Wood
Circus Train Top
(Ohio Art)
5 1/2" x 5"
$15

Right: Tin & Wood
Figural Clown Top
7" Dia. x 9 1/2"
$45

Left: Tin & Wood Clowns
& Geometric Designs Top
(J. Chein & Co.)
6 1/2" Dia. x 5 1/2"
$15

Right: Tin & Wood
"Clowns & the Big Top"
Top
4 1/2" Dia. x 4 1/2"
$40

Left: Tin & Plastic Clown Face
Bubble Top
(LBZ; 1961)
7 1/2" Dia. x 9"
{Note Eyes & Tongue Move}
$35

Right: Tin & Wood
Zebra Top
(Ohio Art)
5 1/2" Dia. x 5"
$25

Left: Tin & Wood
"Animals & Stars" Top
(Ohio Art)
9" Dia. x 8 1/2"
$10

Right: Tin & Wood
"Buggy Garden" Top
(LBZ)
6" Dia. x 5 1/2"
$15

Left: Tin & Wood "Playful
Puppies" Top
5" Dia. x 5"
$10

Right: Tin & Wood
"Dog & Cat & Mouse"
Top
(Ohio Art)
7" Dia. x 7"
$20

Left: Tin & Wood
"Baseball Bears" Top
5" Dia. x 5 1/2"
$25

Right: Tin & Plastic
"Sleepy Teddy Top"
(Ohio Art)
7" Dia. x 6"
$15

Left: Tin & Wood
"Birds & Butterflies"
5 1/2" Dia. x 5"
$10

Right: Tin & Wood
"Jungle Animals" Top
5 1/2" Dia. x 5"
$10

Left: Tin & Wood
"Spanish Children" Top
(Ohio Art)
7" Dia. x 7 1/4"
$10

Above: Tin & Wood "Tri-Level" Top
6" Dia. x 8"
$45

Above: Tin & Plastic Butterfly Top
(LBZ Co.)
7" Dia. x 7"
$30

Left: Tin & Wood
"Frolicking Children" Top
5 1/2" Dia. x 5"
$10

Right: Tin & Wood
"Space Scene" Top
5 1/2" Dia. x 5"
$15

Left: Tin & Wood
"Humming" Top
(Wyandotte Toys)
5 1/2" Dia. x 5 1/2"
$20

Above: Tin & Wood "Street People" Top
5 1/2" Dia. x 8 1/2"
$35

Above: Tin & Wood "Child Pilots" Top
(Ohio Art)
6 1/2" Dia. x 6 1/2"
$15

Above: Tin & Wood "Country Kids" Top
(Ohio Art)
7" Dia. x 7"
$15

Above: Tin & Wood "Drag Race" Top
(Ohio Art)
9 1/2" Dia. x 10"
$25

Right: Tin & Wood
"Musical Children" Top
(Wyandotte Toys)
8 3/4" Dia. x 9"
$30

Left: Tin & Wood
Geometric Design Top
5 1/2" Dia. x 5"
$5

Right: Aluminum Humming
Top "Волчок"
(Made in Soviet Union)
5 1/2" Dia. x 6"
$35 with box

Left: Tin & Wood
"Choral Top"
(Made in Germany)
4 1/2" Dia. x 7"
$150+ with box

Right: Tin & Wood
Multi-Colored Top
5 1/2" Dia. x 9"
$30

Left: Small Tin & Wood Top
2 1/2" Dia. x 3"
$15

Above: Tin & Wood Musical Bell Top
(Ohio Art)
8 1/2" Dia. x 9"
$25

Above: Tin & Wood Bell Top
8 1/2" Dia. x 11"
$20

Top Related Items

Left: "Whirl, Spin the Top Game"
(B.S. & Co. of Japan)
3 3/4" Dia.
$30 complete

Above & Below: Peg Top Game
(Parker Brothers)
12" x 12"
$40 complete

Above: Mechanical Top
(J. Chein & Co.)
7 1/4" Dia. x 7 1/2"
$35

Above: "Electro Rainbow Top"
(Shawnee Novelty Manufacturing Co.)
3 1/2" Dia. x 4"
{Note Handheld Plastic Launcher}
$35 with box

Above: "Best Maid" Topset
(Made in Japan)
Tops: 2 1/2" Dia. x 1/2"
$75 complete

Right: Multi-Color Top
(C.E. Carter Co.)
6" Dia.
{Note Model #25}
$75 with box

Above: Tin "Flicker Top"
4 1/4" Dia.
{Note: Patented 1920}
$15

Left: Plastic Robot Top w/ Hand Launcher
(Made in Hong Kong)
3 3/4" tall
$10

Below: Tin Top "Blow on it-
See it Spin"
1 3/4" Dia.
$5

Above: Tin Top "Blow on it-
See it Spin"
2" Dia.
$5

Below: "Shoot-A-Top" Set
Wooden Peg Tops: 1 1/2" Dia. x 2"
Plastic Launchers: 4 1/4" long
$45 set

Wooden Yo-Yos

Above: Wooden Yo-Yo
(Made in Japan)
2 3/4" Dia. x 1 1/2"
$10

Below: Large Wooden Yo-Yo
4" Dia.
$15

Above: VIP Wooden Yo-Yo
3 1/2" Dia.
$15

Left: Wooden Floral Yo-Yo
2 1/4" Dia.
{Note: Also Contains Plastic
& Metal Pieces}
$35

Right: "Genuine Goody
Filipino Twirler"
$35

Left: Whirl-King Standard Model
Average Size
$10

Right: Royal Champion
Junior Top
Average Size
$10

Left: Champion Return Top -
Style 55
2" Dia.
$10

Right: Whirl-King Top -
Standard Model
Average Size
$10

Right: Fli-Back Top
Average Size
{Note: Graphics
Appear on Both Sides}
$15

Left: Fli-Back Yo-Yo
Average Size
$10

Right: Flying Disc
(Alox Mfg. Co.)
Average Size
$10

Left: "Big Zapper" Festival
Yo-Yo
(Made in Sweden)
Average Size
$20

Right: Small Wooden Yo-Yo
1 1/4" Dia.
$5

Metal Yo-Yos

Above Pictures: Tin Yo-Yo (Ball Bearing Inside; Both Sides Shown)
(Made in Japan)
1 1/2" Dia.
$5

Left: Tin Global Yo-Yo
(Made in China)
Average Size
$5

Right: Tin Litho Yo-Yo
(Made in China)
Average Size
$5

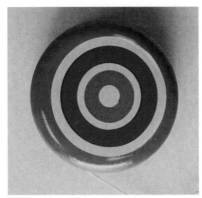

Left: Tin & Steel
Festival Screamer
Average Size
$25

Left: Tin Psychedelic
Litho Yo-Yo
(Made in Hong Kong)
Average Size
$15

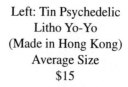

Right: Sterling Silver Yo-Yo
w/ Steel Body
(Gorham Sterling Cove)
Average Size
$90+

Left: Silverplated Yo-Yo
(Towle)
Average Size
$30

Right: Graham Bal-Yo
Average Size
$10

Plastic Yo-Yos

Left: Plastic All-American
Yo-Yo
Average Size
$5

Right: All-Star Champion
Festival Yo-Yo
Average Size
$10

Left: Champion Yo-Yo
(Made in China)
Average Size
$5

Right: Transparent Pink
Yo-Yo
Average Size
$5

Left: Official League Yo-Yo -
Festival Professional Model
2 1/8" Dia.
$20

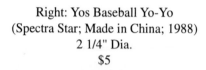

Right: Yos Baseball Yo-Yo
(Spectra Star; Made in China; 1988)
2 1/4" Dia.
$5

Left: Bowler Yo-Yo-
Festival Professional Model
2 1/8" Dia.
$20

Right: Official League
Football Yo-Yo - Festival
Professional Model
1 3/4" Dia. x 3 1/4"
$20

Left: Yellow Yo-Yo
(Jaru)
Average Size
$10

Right: Yos '57 Chevy Yo-Yo
(Spectra Star; Made in China; 1989)
Average Size
$10

Left: Yos "Boom" Yo-Yo
(Spectra Star; Made in China; 1988)
Average Size
$5

Right: Butterfly Shaped Super
Return Race Wheel
Average Size
$10

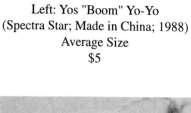

Duncan Yo-Yos

Left: Duncan Beginner Yo-Yo
1 7/8" Dia.
$10

Right: Genuine Duncan
Beginner's Yo-Yo
Average Size
$10

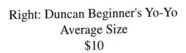

Left: Genuine Beginner's Yo-Yo
1 3/4" Dia.
$10

Right: Duncan Beginner's Yo-Yo
Average Size
$10

Left: Duncan Gold Award
Average Size
$10

Right: Genuine Duncan
Yo-Yo - Gold Award
Average Size
$10

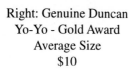

Left: Genuine Duncan Yo-Yo -
Gold Award
Average Size
$10

Right: Duncan Professional
Average Size
$15

Left: Duncan Professional
Average Size
$10

Right: Duncan Professional Yo-Yo
Average Size
$10

Below: Duncan Imperial Yo-Yo
2 1/4" Dia.
$15 with package

Left: Duncan Imperial
Average Size
$10

Above: Duncan Imperial
Average Size
$10

Left: Duncan Glow Imperial
Average Size
$10

Left: Duncan Glow Imperial
2 1/4" Dia.
$15 with card

Left: Duncan Mel-YO-Dee
Average Size
$15

Right: Duncan Satellite
Yo-Yo Return Top
Average Size
$10

Left: Ducan Junior Yo-Yo Return Top
1 1/4" Dia.
$5

Right: Duncan Velvet
Average Size
$15

Left: The General Lee
(Butterfly Shaped)
Average Size
$35

Right: Duncan Long Spin Wheels
(Butterfly Shaped)
Average Size
$20

Left: Duncan Midnight Special
Average Size
$10

Right: Duncan "Wood Grain"
Average Size
$15

Left: Duncan Jeweled Cat's Eye
Average Size
$20

Right: Duncan Jeweled Eagle's Eye
Average Size
$20

Left: Genuine Duncan
Butterfly Yo-Yo
Average Size
$10

Right: Duncan Special
Average Size
$5

Left: 300 Don Duncan
2 1/4" Dia.
$30

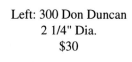

Right: Wooden Duncan
Yo-Yo Return Top
Average Size
$15

Left: Duncan Tops Yo-Yo
Average Size
$10

Right: Duncan Jeweled
Tournament Yo-Yo Tops
{Note: Variations have 4
or 5 Jewels}
Average Size
$20

Right: Duncan Bowling
Ball Yo-Yo Return Top
2 1/4" Dia.
{Note: Model #2100;
Graphics Read "Amflite
AMF Bowling Balls}
$15 on card

Right: Duncan
Tournament Yo-Yo
Return Top
2 1/4" Dia.
{Note: Model
#1077}
$15 on card

Left: Duncan Satellite
Lighted Yo-Yo
2 1/4" Dia.
{Note: Model #3268}
$15

Below: Duncan Mark II - Shrieking Sonic Satellite Yo-Yo
2 1/4" Dia.
{Note: Model #500}
$20 on card

Wood & Metal Advertising Yo-Yos

Right: Painted Steel Yo-Yo
[Bosco 3-Food Drink]
2" Dia.
$40

Above: Tin Advertising Yo-Yo
[Buster Brown Shoes]
(Made in Japan; Both Sides Shown)
Average Size
$30

Right: Wooden Yo-Yo
[Drink Coca-Cola In Bottles]
(Edwards Mfg. Co.; 1930's)
1 3/4" Dia.
$75+

Above: Wooden Advertising Yo-Yo
[50 Years of Dependability- Dodge - 1914-1964]
(Both Sides Shown)
1 3/4" Dia.
$20

Left: Duncan Beginner's Yo-Yo
[Ever Sweet Orange Juice]
Average Size
$15

Above: Wooden Advertising Yo-Yo
[GE - General Electric}
2 1/4" Dia.
$25

Right: Wooden Advertising
Yo-Yo
[Kist Beverages]
Average Size
{Note: Graphics Appear on
Both Sides}
$20

Left: Wooden Advertising Yo-Yo
[Tastee-Freez]
Average Size
$15

Right: Wooden Advertising
Yo-Yo
[Toys-R-Us]
$15

Plastic Advertising Yo-Yos

Above: Advertising Yo-Yo
[Amoco]
Average Size
$10

Above: Advertising Yo-Yo
(Duracraft, Inc)
[Bellevue Center- "Greatest
Yo on Earth"]
(Both Sides Shown)
Average Size
$5

Left: Burger Chef & Jeff Yo-Yo
[Burger Chef]
Average Size
{Note: Copyright 1972}
$15

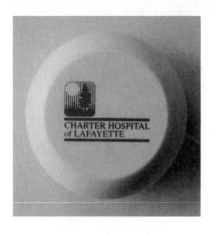

Left: Advertising Yo-Yo
[Charter Hospital of Lafayette]
Average Size
$5

Right: Chuck E. Cheese
[Showbiz Pizza Time, Inc.; 1991]
(Made in Hong Kong)
Average Size
{Note: SN#2200}
$5

Left: "Galaxy" Genuine
Russell Yo-Yo
[Coca-Cola]
(Made in Philippines; 1980)
Average Size
$10

Right: Russell Royale
"Galaxy 200" Return Top
[Drink Coca-Cola]
(Made in Philipines)
Average Size
$10

Right: Duncan Imperial
[Enjoy Coca-Cola; 1970's]
Average Size
$15

Left: Advertising Yo-Yo
[Drink Coca-Cola; 1960's]
1 3/4" Dia.
$25

Right: Advertising Yo-Yo
[Drink Coca-Cola]
1 1/2" Dia.
$5

Left: Big Chief Tournament Yo-Yo
[Coleman's Sausage]
(Plastic & Metal)
Average Size
$10

81

Above: Advertising Yo-Yo
[Customer Care]
Average Size
$5

Above: Duncan Imperial
[Express Delta - Delta Airlines]
Average Size
$10

Right: Advertising Yo-Yo
[Exide Batteries]
Average Size
$10

Left: Advertising Yo-Yo
[Ford Trucks]
Average Size
$10

Right: Advertising Yo-Yo
[B.F. Goodrich]
1 3/4" Dia.
$10

Left: Tournament Yo-Yo
[Hardee's Restaurants]
(Sayco)
$10

Below: Duncan Butterfly
[Honey & Nut Corn Flakes]
Average Size
$20

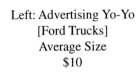

Right: Advertising Yo-Yo
[Integrated Business Systems]
Average Size
$5

Above: Duncan Imperial
[Leader Drug Stores]
(Both Sides Shown)
Average Size
$10

Below: Advertising Yo-Yo
[Long John Silver's Restaurants]
(Made in China)
Average Size
$10

Left: Advertising Yo-Yo
[McDonald's Corp.]
Average Size
$5

Right: Morton Yo-Nut
[Morton Donuts]
2 1/2" Dia.
$10

Above: Tiny Advertising Yo-Yo
[Pizza Hut Restaurants]
(Made in Hong Kong)
1 1/8" Dia.
$5

Below: Advertising Yo-Yo
[Oreo Cookies]
2 1/8" Dia.
$15

Left: Advertising Yo-Yo
[Plan America]
Average Size
$5

Above: Duncan Glow Imperial
[Rice Krispies]
Average Size
$10

Above: Advertising Yo-Yo
[Scientific - On the Road Again]
Average Size
$10

Above: Advertising Yo-Yo
[Seneca Wire]
Average Size
$5

Above: Advertising Yo-Yo
[Southside Recycled Plastics]
Average Size
$5

Above: Duncan Imperial
[Wendy's Restaurants]
Average Size
$10

Right: Advertising Yo-Yo
[Wood Lake Reservation -
Boy Scouts of America]
Average Size
$10

Left: Advertising Yo-Yo
[Wyoming Coal - W.R.D.]
Average Size
$5

Character Yo-Yos

Above: Tiny Plastic Yo-Yo
[Alvin the Chipmunk]
(Made in Taiwan)
1 1/8" Dia.
$10

Left: Plastic Yos Yo-Yo
[Batman]
(Spectra Star; 1989)
Average Size
$10 with card

Above: Duncan Butterfly
[Batman & Robin; 1978]
Average Size
$25

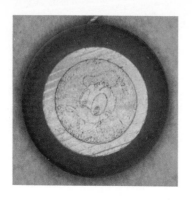

Left: Wooden Yo-Yo
[Donald Duck]
$30

Right: Plastic Yos Yo-Yo
[Donald Duck]
(Spectra Star; Made in China; 1988)
Average Size
$5

Left: Plastic Yo-Yo
[Fred Flintstone]
(Made in Hong Kong)
Average Size
$15

Right: Plastic Yo-Yo
[Garfield the Cat]
(Avon Products, Inc. & Spectra Star;
Made in China; 1981)
2 1/4" Dia.
$5 with card

Left: Plastic Yos Yo-Yo
[G.I. Joe]
(Spectra Star; 1988)
Average Size
$5

Right: Tin Yo-Yo
[Oliver Hardy]
(Made in Hong Kong;
1976)
$25

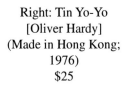

Left: Plastic Yos Yo-Yo
[The Joker]
(Spectra Star; Made in China; 1989)
Average Size
$5

Right: Plastic Yo-Yo
[Linus Van Pelt]
Average Size
$15

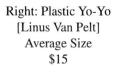

Above: Duncan Imperial Jr. Yo-Yo Return Top
[Mickey Mouse]
(Both Sides Shown)
Average Size
$40

Left: Duncan Yo-Yo
Return Top
[Official Mickey
Mouse Club]
2" Dia.
{Note: Model #1451}
$55 on card

Right: Plastic Yo-Yo
[Mickey Mouse]
Average Size
$15

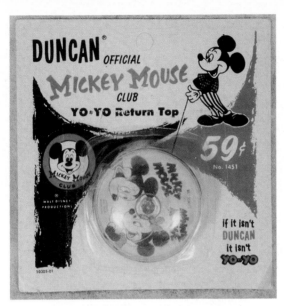

Above: Duncan Yo-Yo Return Top
[Mickey Mouse & Minnie Mouse]
Average Size
$55 on card

Left: Disney Yo-Yo for Beginners
[Mickey Mouse]
(Hallmark Cards, Inc.)
2" Dia.
$10

Right: Plastic Yos Yo-Yo
[Pee Wee Herman]
(Spectra Star; Made in China; 1988)
2 1/4" Dia.
$10

Above: "Roundup King" Top
[Roy Rogers & Trigger]
(Western Plastics, Inc.)
Average Size
$25

Right: Plastic Yo-Yo
[Fighter Pilot Snoopy]
Average Size
$10

Left: Plastic Butterfly-
Style Yo-Yo
[Joe Cool - Snoopy]
Average Size
$10

Above: Tiny Plastic Duncan Yo-Yo
(Sugar Bear - Super Sugar Crisp Cereal)
1 1/2" Dia.
$10

Above & Right: Duncan
Hologram Yo-Yo
[Superman]
Average Size
$20

Left: Plastic Duncan Yo-Yo
[Superman]
$10

Left: Plastic Yos Yo-Yo
[Teenage Mutant Ninja Turtles]
(Spectra Star; Made in China;
1989)
Average Size
$5

Right: Tin Litho
Witch Yo-Yo
(OTC)
Average Size
$5

Left: Plastic Yo-Yo
[Yogi Bear]
(Made in Hong Kong)
Average Size
$15

Right: Wooden Yo-Yo
[Yo-Yo Man - Smothers Brothers]
Average Size
$10

96

Yo-Yo Related Items

Left: Packaged Assortment of
Duncan Yo-Yo Replacement
Strings
5" x 3"
$3 each

Right: Duncan
Spinning Top Spares
3 1/8" x 4 3/4"
$10

Below: Duncan's Genuine Gold Seal
Official Egyptian Fibre Yo-Yo Top Strings
(Copyright 1937)
5 3/4" x 3 1/2"
$15

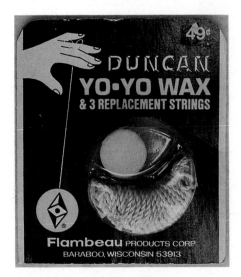

Left: Duncan Yo-Yo Wax &
Three Replacement Strings
4" x 4 1/2"
$5

Right: Display Box of
Fli-Back Yo-Yo Sleeper
Types
(Sock It Co.)
$55 with display

Above: Duncan Yo-Yo Tourney
"Expert" Forward Pass
3/4" Dia.
$10

Left: Various Yo-Yo
Tournament Patches
$20 - 35 each

Above: Official World Champion
Supersonic Yo-Yo Package
12" x 16" Display
$30 with display

Right: Smothers Brothers
Video & Yo-Yo
(Eastman Kodak Co./ Yo-Yo by
Hummingbird Toy Co.; 1988)
$15

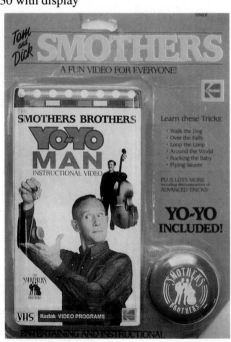

Above: (Left)
Duncan Spinning Top &
Handball Tricks Guide
(Copyright 1962)
7" x 5"
$10

Above: (Right)
Giant Book of Duncan Yo-
Yo Tricks
(Copyright 1961)
7" x 5"
$10

Above: Duncan Book "How to
Master Championship Tricks..."
(Copyright 1947)
$45

Gyroscopes

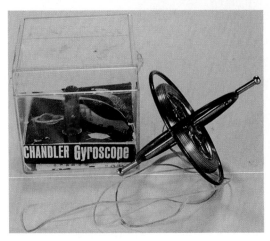

Left: Chandler
Gyroscope
2 1/2" Dia.
$25 with box

Right: All Metal Gyroscope
(Dandy; Patented 1923)
2 1/2" Dia.
$15

Below: The Hurst Gyroscope
(Chandler Mfg. Co.)
3" Dia. x 3 1/2"
$20 with box

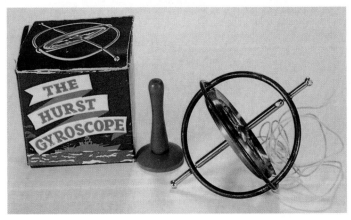

Left: Sputnik Jr.
(Stevens Mfg. Co.; 1957)
2 1/2" Dia.
$25

Above: Saturn Micro Ball Bearing Gyroscope Top
(Paul Henry Co.)
$25

Left: Metal Gyroscope
3" Dia.
$5

Left: Steven's Giant
Gyroscope
(Steven Mfg. Co.; 1963)
$25 with box

Right: Heart-Shaped Gyroscope
$35

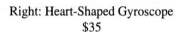

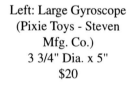

Left: Large Gyroscope
(Pixie Toys - Steven
Mfg. Co.)
3 3/4" Dia. x 5"
$20

Right: Copper &
Aluminum Gyroscope
2" Dia.
$10

Above: Hurst Gyroscope
(Chandler Mfg. Co.)
3"Dia. x 3 1/2"
$20 with box

Right: All Metal Gyroscope
(Gardner; 1909)
3" Dia.
$30

Left: Cast Brass Top
2" x 3"
$75+

105

Above: Gyros Boxed Set - Magnetic
Top & Tin Figural Items
(Made in Germany)
Gyro: 2" Dia.
$50+

Below: Saturn Gyro-Scope Tops
(Burcham Products)
3" Dia. x 3 1/4"
Display: 9 1/4" x 12 1/4"
$50+

Above: All Metal Gyroscope
(Dandy; Patented in 1923)
2 1/2 Dia.
$15

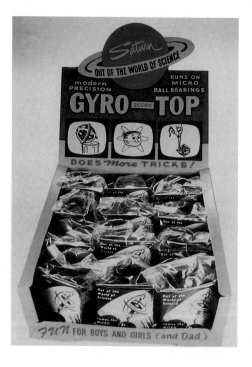

Miscellaneous Spinning Toys

Above: Atomic Jet Flying-O-Saucer
(Tin & Copper)
6" Dia.
$10

Above: Wizzzer Plastic Gyrating Top
[Mattel; 1975]
2 1/4" Dia. x 3"
$10

Right: Whirlaway
(Plastic Flying Spin Toy)
Propellers - 5" Dia.
Launcher - 5" Long
$15

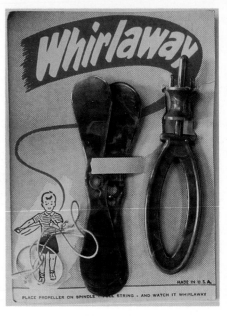

Left: Tin Push Top w/ Dragonfly
Design
[Marklin; Made in Germany]
Top: 3" Dia.
Pump: 7" Long
$50+

Right: Wood & Aluminum
Roto-Jets
["Jolly Jimmy" Toy; 1957]
5 1/8" Wingspan x 6" Long
$35

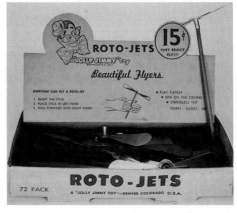

Left: Reversible Tin
& Wood Spin Toy
7 1/2" x 11"
$100+

Right: Wooden Whiptop
[Made in Germany]
18" Whip
$30

Below: Advertising Spinning Stick Game
(Similar to a Diablo)
(Advertising Coca Cola; 1930's)
$75+

Left: Tin Adv.
Helio Jet
(Dad's Root
Beer)
7 3/4" Long
$25

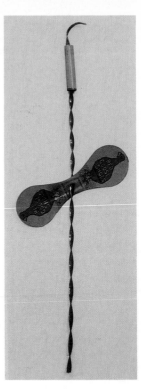

Right: Tin Adv.
Helio Jet
(Red Goose
Shoes)
8" Long
$25

Left: Tin Spinner
[Made in Japan]
6" Long
$15

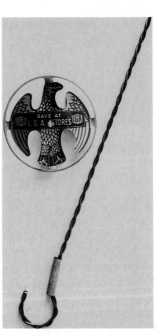

Right: Tin Adv.
Helio Jet
[Lou Fox]
(I.G.A. Stores)
9" Long
$30

Left: Tin Spinner
11 1/2" Long
$15

Right: Steel &
Paper Spiro-Top
(Sunshine Toy Co.)
Disc: 3" Dia.
$20 with card

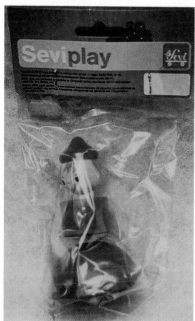

Left: Wooden Stringed
Spinning Figure
(Sevi; Made in Italy)
4" Tall
{Note: String Release
Hidden above Skirt}
$5

Above: Zing Zong
[Made in U.S.A]
3" Dia x 1"
$20

Above: Character Zing Zong
(Snow White & the Seven Dwarfs; 1938)
3 1/2" Dia. x 1"
$75+

Right: Skytop
[Turbo Toy Co.]
4 1/2" Dia.
$10